Other books by Mick Inkpen:

One Bear at Bedtime
The Blue Balloon
Billy's Beetle
Penguin Small
Lullabyhullaballoo!
Nothing
Bear
The Great Pet Sale
Baggy Brown
We are Wearing Out the Naughty Step
This is My Book

The Wibbly Pig books
The Kipper books
The Blue Nose Island books

First published in 1990
by Hodder Children's Books.
This edition published in 2007

Copyright © Mick Inkpen 1990

Hodder Children's Books
338 Euston Road, London NW1 3BH

Hodder Children's Books Australia
Level 17/207 Kent Street, Sydney, NSW 2000

The right of Mick Inkpen to be identified as the author
and illustrator of this Work has been asserted by him in
accordance with the Copyright, Designs and Patents Act 1988.

A catalogue record of this book is
available from the British Library.

ISBN: 9780340931097
10 9 8 7 6 5

Printed in China

Hodder Children's Books is a
division of Hachette Children's Books.
An Hachette UK Company
www.hachette.co.uk

Threadbear

MICK INKPEN

Hodder
Children's
Books

A division of Hachette Children's Books

Ben's bear was called Threadbear. He was old. Bits of him had worn out. Or worked loose. Or dropped off.

He had a paw which didn't match and a button for an eye. When he looked through the button he saw four pictures instead of one. It was like looking in a television shop window.

But there was one thing that had always been wrong with Threadbear. The silly man who had made him had put too much stuffing inside him. His arms were too hard. His legs were too hard. And there was so much stuffing inside his tummy that his squeaker had been squashed.

It had never squeaked. Not even once.

Threadbear hated having a sqeaker in his tummy that wouldn't squeak. It made him feel that he was letting Ben down.

Ben's frog could croak. His space monster could squelch. And his electronic robot could burble away for hours if its batteries were the right way round.

Even the little toy that Ben called Grey Thing could make a noise, and nobody knew what Grey Thing was meant to be!

Nobody could make Threadbear's squeaker work.

Ben's dad couldn't do it.

His mum couldn't do it.

Nor could his auntie or his grandma.

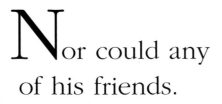

Nor could any
of his friends.

When Ben had measles he asked the doctor about Threadbear's squeaker.
The doctor listened to Threadbear's tummy. But there was no squeak. Not even the faintest sign of one.

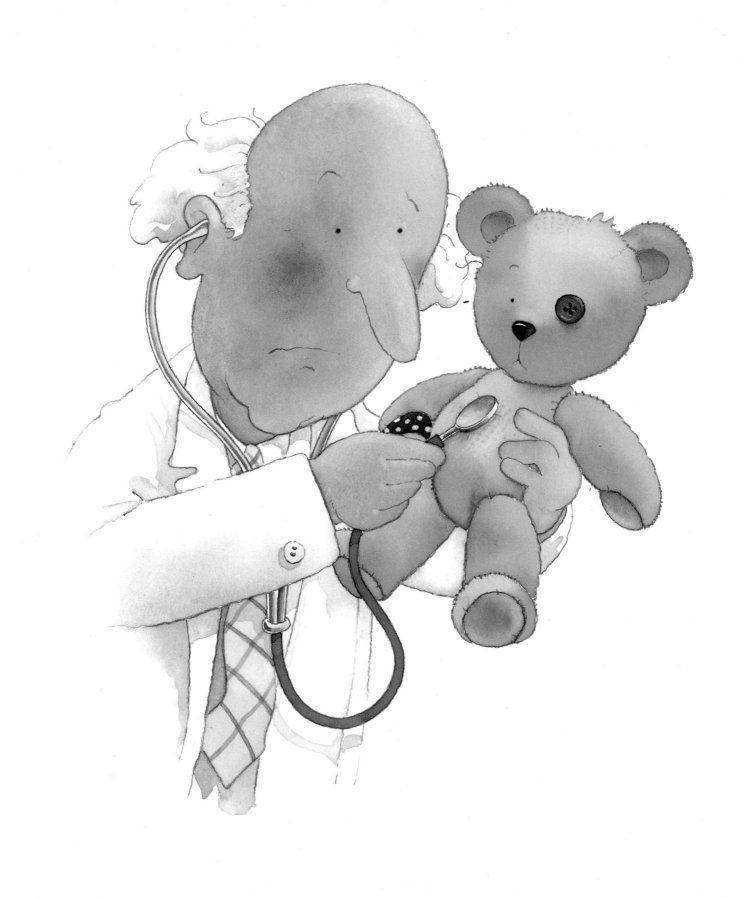

The other toys tried to help.

'If you had a winder like me, we could wind you up,' said Frog.

'If you were made of rubber like me, we could squelch you,' said the space monster.

'If you had batteries like me, we could turn you on,' said the robot. It was not much help.

'Why don't you ask Father Christmas?' said Grey Thing. 'He knows all about toys.' This was a brilliant idea and Grey Thing went a little pink.

'But where does Father Christmas live?' asked Threadbear.

'At a place called the North Pole,' said Grey Thing. 'You can get to it up the chimney, I think.'

Threadbear had never climbed up a chimney before. It was hard work. He took a wrong turn and fell back down.

But he did not give up.

It was long after bedtime when Threadbear poked his head out of the chimney pot.

This must be the North Pole!

Threadbear sat down to wait for Father Christmas. He waited and waited. But Father Christmas did not seem to be coming.

The moon rose into the sky and Threadbear began to doze…

Suddenly Father Christmas was there
helping Threadbear into his sleigh!

T hreadbear felt himself
falling and falling…

Bump! Threadbear woke up. He rubbed his eyes and looked around. There was no squeaker fruit, no squeaker tree and worst of all no Father Christmas.

'I must have fallen asleep and dropped off the North Pole!' said Threadbear.

In the morning Ben was surprised to find Threadbear in the garden covered with soot. Ben's mum put Threadbear straight into the washing machine. She did not even look at the label on Threadbear's neck which read in capital letters 'DO NOT WASH!'

When Threadbear came out of the washing machine the soot was gone, but there was a curious purple stain on his chin, which nobody could explain.

Threadbear was feeling too giddy to notice. His head felt like a spinning top!

'I don't mind feeling giddy,' thought
Threadbear as he hung on the line.
'I don't mind having a button for an
eye and a paw that doesn't match.
I don't even mind being hung up by the
ear. But what I DO mind, what I mind
VERY MUCH is having a silly
squeaker in my tummy
that won't squeak!'

Threadbear was so cross that he
frightened a robin. It flew away leaving
him alone in the garden bouncing angry
little bounces on the washing line.

The sun rose slowly over the garden.
It shone straight down on Threadbear,
a great warm shine like an enormous hug.
Threadbear began to steam. He began to
feel better. The more he steamed the
better he felt.

   He swung his legs backwards and
forwards. Then he kicked them high in the
air. Soon he was swinging round and round
the washing line giggling to himself.

   'Why do I feel so happy?' he wondered.

It was at this moment that Threadbear
realised a very odd thing had happened to
him. His paws felt different. So did his arms
and his legs. They were no longer hard!

And inside his tummy was a wonderful,
loose, comfortable feeling that he had
never felt before!

At the very same moment something
caught Threadbear's eye. Something red was
racing across the sun. And to Threadbear's
surprise the red something was waving goodbye!

When Ben came out to
see if Threadbear was dry
he noticed that his little
brown bear had changed.
   'Look mum,' said Ben,
'he's gone floppy!'
Ben's mum unpegged
Threadbear's ear.
      'Oh dear!' she said. 'His
stuffing must have shrunk in the wash!'
Ben looked at Threadbear.
'I like him like that. It makes him look…'
But Ben could not think of the right word so
instead he gave Threadbear a squeeze.
      And for the first time the squeaker
in Threadbear's tummy gave the
      loudest,
         clearest,
            squeakiest…

...squeak!

Because Baggy Brown was made to celebrate the first birthday of her Royal Highness Princess Sophinyiniannia, first-born and daughter to the King and Queen of Thingland.

First published in 2007
This paperback edition first published in 2013
by Hodder Children's Books.

Copyright © Mick Inkpen 2007

Hodder Children's Books
338 Euston Road, London, NW1 3BH

Hodder Children's Books Australia
Level 17/207 Kent Street, Sydney, NSW 2000

The right of Mick Inkpen to be identified as the author
and illustrator of this Work has been asserted by him in
accordance with the Copyright, Designs and Patents Act 1988.

A catalogue record of this book is
available from the British Library.

ISBN: 978 1 444 91646 1
10 9 8 7 6 5 4 3 2 1

Printed in Italy

Hodder Children's Books is a
division of Hachette Children's Books,
an Hachette UK Company
www.hachette.co.uk

Baggy Brown
and the Royal Baby
the

Mick Inkpen

Hodder
Children's
Books

A division of Hachette Children's Books

P rincess Sophinyiniannia, (Sophie for short), also started out well, as you can imagine.

To give you some idea, this is just the top of the pile of cuddly toys that arrived for her the very day she was born.

But do you know, not one of them could stop her crying. Week after week her little howls rang right royally throughout the palace.

In fact her cries were so upsetting that the King and Queen had to pull their crowns over their ears!

At this time Baggy Brown was not called Baggy Brown at all, but just No.1, which was the number stamped on the little gold crown in his ear.

He was the first of the 1000 special bears and the only one, *the only one*, without a price tag. He was priceless, you see, because he was to be presented to Princess Sophie.

And because of this he had a large NOT FOR SALE label slapped on the end of his nose.

Ouch!

It was such a shock that Baggy Brown did not line himself up properly when the big grabbler came round. It missed him completely!

While all the other bears were grabbled and whizzed away, No.1 continued along the conveyor belt and fell straight off the end.

Down he fell, down, down, and back into the very innards of the big red teddy bear machine at Better Bears Ltd.

He was grubbed and fluffed
and plumped and scrodged
and frizzled and squidged
and pummelled and hooshed
and hooshed
and hooshed again!
And when it had finished with
him, the big red teddy bear machine
spat him out onto the factory floor,
where a passing factory worker
called Jack trod on him.

F or three days Alfie carried Baggy Brown everywhere with him. But on the fourth day he hid him, and I will tell you why.

On that day the television news finished with a story about a missing royal bear. 'Number One, first in a long line of bears, is missing!' said the reporter. He was holding up No.2 bear.

'Number One! No.1! That's you Baggy Brown!' said Alfie.

And that is why, almost as soon as Baggy Brown got his real name, he was being stuffed head first into one of Jack's smelly old wellies.

Now Jack wasn't to know that Baggy Brown was a priceless bear. He certainly didn't look like one. So he picked him up and took him home for his young son, Alfie.

Alfie loved Baggy Brown from the moment he saw him. He loved his lopsided face and his soft, saggy body. He loved, too, the strange gold button under Baggy Brown's squashed ear, even though he could make no sense of the name on it.

'No. . . 1?' read Alfie slowly. 'No one is a silly name for a bear.' And he began to think of a proper name.

That night Alfie couldn't sleep. He crept downstairs and rescued Baggy Brown from the stair cupboard. Silently he opened the front door and stepped out into the cool night.

Alfie knew his way through all the narrow alleyways that led down to the banks of The Great River. He knew too all the watery places where the coal barges slopped against the wharves. And he knew exactly which boat would head off into the city before first light.

It was into this that he jumped, curled himself into a ball around Baggy Brown, and fell asleep.

B aggy Brown was wide awake as the barge slipped out into The Great River.

He was awake as it slid under black bridges and winking stars.

He was awake as it sounded its horn, just as it always did when approaching the Royal Palace to drop off its load of coal for the Royal Boiler House.

But all the while Alfie slept on.

W hich is how he was
found by the Royal Stoker.
The Stoker, who did not
have a clue what to do with the
grubby little boy and his grubby little
bear, summoned a Royal Footman.

'This belongs to the Princess!'
said Alfie holding up Baggy Brown.

The Stoker and the Footman
burst into laughter.

'I don't think so, son,' said
the Stoker.

'Don't be ridiculous!'
said the Footman. 'And
take that disgusting
object away!'

But Alfie refused to budge. 'It does!' he said. 'It belongs to the Princess!' So the Footman sent for one of the Ladies in Waiting.

Lady Jane Farque-Hurrah was undaunted by the smell of old welly rising from Baggy Brown. And having five children of her own, she knew exactly when a child was telling the truth.

She examined Baggy Brown closely. As she lifted his coal black ear there was a bright glint of gold.

'Aha!' she said, and read aloud, 'No.1!'

'His name is Baggy Brown,' said Alfie.

After a quick clean up with Lady Jane Farque-Hurrah's hanky, Alfie was led through the Palace to the Royal Nursery where Princess Sophie was howling as usual.

Sophie looked at Alfie.
She looked at Baggy Brown.
She stopped crying!
And for the first time in fifty-three weeks the Royal Palace was quiet.

Sadly Alfie pushed Baggy Brown through the bars of the Royal Cot and was led away. But at this moment Sophie started to howl even louder than before!

'Alfie,' whispered Lady Jane, 'it's not Baggy Brown that Sophie wants. . .

. . . it's you!'

S o that sealed it. Alfie was allowed to keep Baggy Brown, which of course meant that Baggy Brown was allowed to keep Alfie.

And what about Sophie?
Well the following week a parcel arrived for Alfie. In it was a silver phone with just one golden  button. From that day on, whenever he liked, Alfie could call for the Royal Barge to take him and his friends up The Great River to the Royal Palace to visit Sophie.

This is them in the treehouse that the King had built in the Palace Garden when Sophie was five and Alfie was nine.

And if I had longer to tell you what happened, I would tell you that Sophie loved Alfie and his baggy brown bear for the rest of her life, and married him just after her 21st birthday.

I would tell you that Alfie's father, Jack, became the proud owner of Better Bears Ltd, but his proudest day was the day he learned that his grandson, future King of Thingland, was to be named after him.

I would tell you that on the day His Royal Highness Prince Jack was born, 10,000 bears rolled off the conveyor belt at Better Bears Ltd. . .

. . . and I would tell you that
none of them was loved as
much as Baggy Brown.